COOL RIDES THAT FLY

HOVERBIKES, HIGH-SPEED HELICOPTERS, AND MORE

by Tammy Gagne

CAPSTONE PRESS
a capstone imprint

Capstone Captivate is published by Capstone Press,
an imprint of Capstone.
1710 Roe Crest Drive, North Mankato, Minnesota, 56003
www.capstonepub.com

Copyright © 2021 by Capstone. All rights reserved. No part of this publication may be reproduced in whole or in part, or stored in a retrieval system, or transmitted in any form or by any means, electronic, mechanical, photocopying, recording, or otherwise, without written permission of the publisher.

Library of Congress Cataloging-in-Publication Data is available on the Library of Congress website.
ISBN: 978-1-4966-8361-8 (library binding)
ISBN: 978-1-4966-8412-7 (eBook PDF)

Summary: Describes unique and interesting vehicles that fly, including flying cars, high-speed helicopters, UAVs, and more.

Image Credits
Boeing Management Company, Cover, 19; Newscom: Cover Images/Aeromobil/S_Photo, 22, Cover Images/Opener, 20, MEGA/Hoversurf.com, 25, Polaris, 13 (Bottom), Polaris/Solar Impulse, 7, REUTERS/Andrew Innerarity, 17, SIPA/Global News/J. REVILLARD, 6, TASS/Marina Lystseva, 21, TERRAFUGIA/MAVRIXONLINE.COM, 23, WENN.com/ZOB/CB2, 27, ZUMA Press/MarsScientific Trumbull, 11; Shutterstock: Costazzurra, 5, 29, u3d, 28; U.S. Air Force graphic, 9, U.S. Air Force photo by Chad Bellay, 8; U.S. Marine Corps photo by Cpl. Nathan Reyes, 16, Lance Cpl. Seth Rosenberg, 15; U.S. Navy photo by Mass Communication Specialist 1st Class Peter D. Lawlor, 12, Mass Communication Specialist 3rd Class Josiah J. Kunkle, 13 (Top), Petty Officer 3rd Class Kyle Goldberg, 14

Design Elements
Capstone; Shutterstock: teerayut tae

Editorial Credits
Editor: Carrie Sheely; Designer: Juliette Peters;
Media Researcher: Jo Miller; Premedia Specialist: Katy LaVigne

All internet sites appearing in back matter were available and accurate when this book was sent to press.

Printed and bound in the USA.
PA117

TABLE OF CONTENTS

Take Flight!... 4
Solar Impulse 2 6
Boeing X-51A WaveRider 8
Virgin Galactic VSS Unity 10
UAVs.. 12
F-35B STOVL Lightning II....................... 14
High-Speed Helicopters............................. 16
Boeing eVTOL 18
Personal Air Vehicles 20
Flying Cars 22
Hoverbikes 24
Carbon Fiber Jet Wing Suit 26
The Future of Aircraft 28

    Glossary 30
    Read More..31
    Internet Sites..31
    Index..32

Words in **bold** are in the glossary.

Take Flight!

Look up! What do you see? Is it a bird? Is it a plane? No, it's a flying car! Long ago, inventors dreamed of vehicles that could fly through the air. As **technology** moved forward, aircraft got better. People now take to the skies in **solar**-powered aircraft and hoverbikes. Some planes can take off without runways. Some aircraft can even fly without a human pilot on board.

Modern technology makes it possible for aircraft to break many records. Some aircraft break speed records. Some fly people farther into space than ever before. Other aircraft are designed differently than any before them. Get the details on some of the coolest aircraft to fly the skies!

Some transportation experts think that people will own flying cars someday.

Solar Impulse 2

Imagine flying around the world using nothing but sunlight for fuel! That's exactly what Bertrand Piccard and André Borschberg did in the Solar Impulse 2. In 2016, it became the first solar airplane to fly around the world.

The Solar Impulse 2 spent 23 days in the air. It traveled more than 25,000 miles (40,200 kilometers). Sunlight charged the plane's battery as it flew during the day. It reached a maximum **altitude** of 28,000 feet (8,534 meters) during the day. At night, the aircraft didn't have sunlight to charge the batteries. It then glided at about 5,000 feet (1,524 m) to help the aircraft save energy.

A test pilot flew Solar Impulse 2 over Hawaii.

André Borschberg (left) and Bertrand Piccard (right) landed in Abu Dhabi, United Arab Emirates, to complete their journey.

The plane's **wingspan** was larger than a jumbo jet's. The wings carried more than 17,000 solar cells. They changed sunlight into energy. The aircraft used this energy to run and charge the batteries.

FACT:
The Solar Impulse 2 flew at an average speed of 46 miles (74 km) per hour. It traveled fastest when the sunlight was bright.

Boeing X-51A WaveRider

The Boeing X-51A WaveRider took speed to an extreme. This experimental unmanned vehicle flew at hypersonic speed. That is five times faster than the speed of sound, or about 3,800 miles (6,116 km) per hour.

As air hits flying aircraft, it slows down the vehicles. This force is called drag. The WaveRider had a pointed nose. Its design cut down on drag. It also used a rocket booster. This engine helped the aircraft gain speed quickly.

A B-52 Stratofortress carried the WaveRider under one of its wings.

an artist's drawing of the WaveRider

A B-52 Stratofortress plane carried the WaveRider into the air for its test flights. It then launched the vehicle. The WaveRider's longest test flight was in 2013. It lasted just 6 minutes, 10 seconds.

The U.S. Air Force worked with aircraft companies to design the WaveRider. It can use what was learned from the project to build future hypersonic weapons in the future.

 **FACT:** At hypersonic speed, you could reach anywhere on Earth in less than three hours!

Virgin Galactic VSS Unity

Would you blast into space on a rocket-powered plane? Virgin Galactic wants to take customers to space one day. The company built a plane called the Virgin Galactic VSS Unity. It has already carried its first passenger. On February 22, 2019, two pilots brought passenger Beth Moses to space.

The 2019 test flight traveled almost 56 miles (90 km) above Earth. The VSS Unity left the ground in California beneath another aircraft. The WhiteKnight Two lifted the Unity about 45,000 feet (13,716 m) before dropping it about an hour later. The Unity's pilots, Dave Mackay and Mike Masucci, then took the controls. They fired the Unity's rocket motor. The aircraft reached a top speed of 2,300 miles (3,701 km) per hour before gliding safely back to Earth.

Hot gases shot out from the VSS Unity as it performed its second rocket-powered test flight in 2018.

 **FACT:**
Riders to space will pay a steep price. Virgin Galactic plans to charge customers about $250,000 per ticket!

UAVs

Some aircraft don't need pilots inside. These include unmanned aerial vehicles (UAVs). Some UAVs are called drones. UAVs are especially useful to militaries. The vehicles can fly into dangerous areas without risking human life.

The Predator C Avenger is one of the U.S. military's most advanced UAVs. It has a top speed of 460 miles (740 km) per hour. It can stay in the air for 18 hours. A pilot controls the UAV remotely from a station on the ground. The station includes a video display, maps, and even a **touchscreen**.

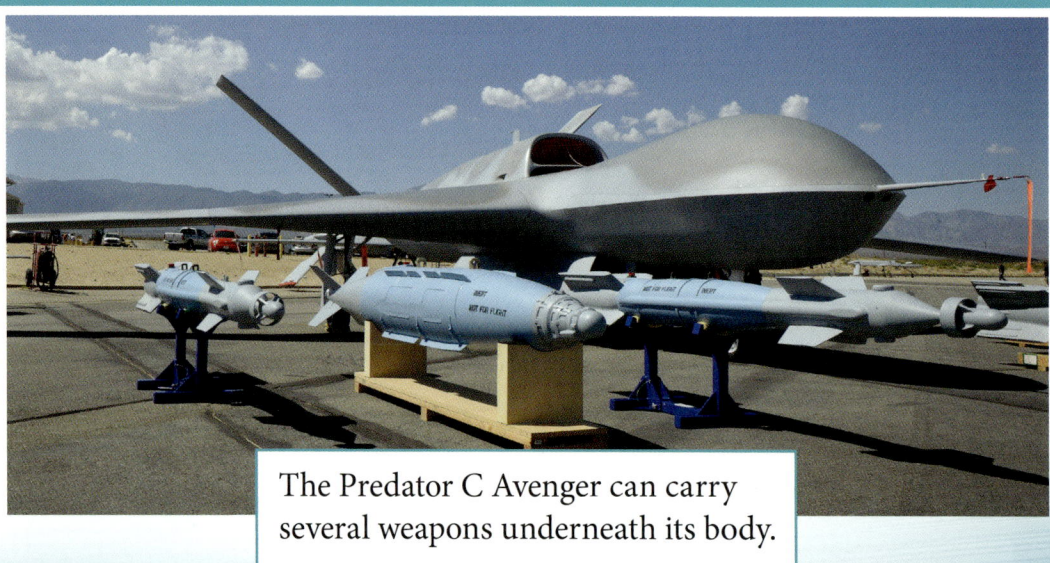

The Predator C Avenger can carry several weapons underneath its body.

A Fire Scout lifts off from a flight deck of a U.S. Navy ship.

The U.S. military also flies the MQ-8C Fire Scout. Pilots can launch this UAV from a ship. It can stay in the air up to 12 hours.

Delivery Drones at Your Door

Drones might soon come right to your door! Companies such as Amazon.com plan to use them to make deliveries to customers. Amazon.com plans for its aircraft to deliver packages less than 5 pounds (2.3 kilograms). The company expects its drones to travel up to 15 miles (24 km). It hopes to get packages to customers in less than 30 minutes.

F-35B STOVL Lightning II

The F-35B STOVL Lightning II doesn't need a long runway. STOVL stands for "short takeoff and vertical landing." The aircraft can lift off the ground from a short airstrip. It can also land without a runway. The F-35B can take off from the smallest air bases. It can even take off from ships in the middle of the ocean.

The F-35B Lightning II's ability to rise vertically helps it lift off quickly from ships.

The F-35B is a **stealth** fighter jet. It is designed to be hard for enemy **radar** systems to find. The body's shape and smoothness keep radar signals from bouncing back to enemy radar systems. The plane also carries weapons and fuel inside its body. These features also make it hard for enemy radar systems to find the plane.

In-Flight Refueling

The F-35B can refuel during flight. Everything has to work just right for this to happen. The pilot moves a long part called a probe from the plane. It attaches to a hose connected to a tanker aircraft. The hose pumps fuel into the F-35B's gas tank.

High-Speed Helicopters

Speed can mean the difference between life and death for people in the military. Fast helicopters can quickly take soldiers into **combat** areas. They can help soldiers get out of dangerous areas. The aircraft can also help get hurt soldiers to hospitals quickly.

The CH-47F Chinook is among the fastest military helicopters in the world. It can reach a speed of 196 miles (315 km) per hour. Sometimes this twin-engine helicopter carries troops. It also carries large weapons and other cargo.

A CH-47F Chinook takes to the air in the Bahamas.

Sikorsky showed off its S-97 Raider helicopter in Jupiter, Florida, in 2014.

The S-97 Raider can go even faster. Its top speed is around 230 miles (370 km) per hour. It can also fly sideways and backward. A pilot can even keep control of the helicopter while it spins. The company that built the helicopter, Sikorsky, continues to improve and test it.

Boeing eVTOL

Imagine you need to get across a big city. You call a taxi service. But a car doesn't come to get you. Instead, a Boeing eVTOL picks you up from the top of a skyscraper!

The Boeing eVTOL is a vertical takeoff and landing aircraft. The aircraft's eight rotors help it lift into the air. A propeller then pushes it forward. The fully electric vehicle runs on battery power. It is built to fly without a human pilot.

Boeing designed a **concept** model of the eVTOL in 2018. One year later, the **prototype** took to the air for a test flight. It took off, hovered, and landed. More test flights are planned for the future. The company hopes that the vehicle will someday be able to carry passengers short distances around big cities.

The eVTOL completed its first flight in January 2019.

Personal Air Vehicles

If you had your own personal air vehicle (PAV), you wouldn't need to call an air taxi service. You could just get in the vehicle and take off. Up, up, and away! PAVs are getting closer to becoming reality. These lightweight planes and helicopters fly lower than larger aircraft.

A company called Opener made the BlackFly. Company leaders hope that it will soon be available for people to buy. They have said it will cost about the same as a sport utility vehicle (SUV). Users will need to complete some training to operate this eVTOL. But U.S. pilots will only need a driver's license to fly it.

The single-seat BlackFly is fully powered by electricity. It can fly about 25 miles (40 km) before needing to be recharged.

The Vahana has four propellers at its front and four in back.

The Airbus A3 Vahana is another eVTOL PAV. It needs no pilot. Advanced sensors can see if another aircraft or a bird is in its path. It then moves around the obstacle.

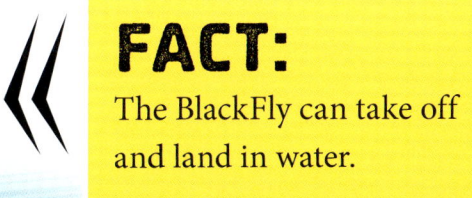

FACT:
The BlackFly can take off and land in water.

Flying Cars

Flying cars have been in books and movies for many years. Today, companies are working to make them a reality. Flying cars combine the abilities of automobiles and airplanes. Their wheels and wings help them go from highway to skyway in a flash!

The AeroMobil is one kind of flying car. It is shaped like a teardrop to help it cut through the air. The wheels fold up for flight. Its wings fold back for land use. The propeller also folds in to use it on land.

The AeroMobil's landing gear folds out for it to land.

The Transition can change between driving and flight mode in less than a minute.

The Terrafugia Transition is another flying car. It looks like a small airplane. It runs on both gasoline and electricity. A boost mode gives the vehicle extra power in the air. Its wings fold up when it drives on land.

Hoverbikes

A hoverbike is like a flying motorcycle. The rider sits on it and holds onto handlebars. But instead of zipping along the ground on wheels, it has propellers that lift it into the air.

The Hoversurf S3 can fly as high as 16 feet (5 m) above the ground. It has a top speed of 60 miles (97 km) per hour. Its electric battery allows the hoverbike to stay in the air for 25 minutes.

British company Malloy Aeronautics is working on a hoverbike that looks like a drone. It can move about as fast as the Hoversurf S3. But it can go much higher—up to 9,987 feet (3,044 m). It can also carry up to 287 pounds (130 kg). This bike is still in the prototype stage. Its builders hope to make it available for military soldiers.

A rider lifts off the ground on a Hoversurf Scorpion-3.

 **FACT:** Hoverbikes are very expensive vehicles. The Hoversurf S3 sells for $150,000.

Carbon Fiber Jet Wing Suit

Yves Rossy can fly with little more than a wing on his back. Rossy designed the Carbon Fiber Jet Wing Suit. It allows him to fly thousands of feet off the ground.

The suit is made of four tiny jet engines. They lift him up after he launches from another aircraft. Rossy has used the suit to fly over both the English Channel and the Grand Canyon. He has even used it to fly in patterns with airplanes.

Rossy has learned to perform tricks such as loops and rolls in the air. When he is done flying, he uses a parachute to reach the ground safely.

Rossy soared through the sky in his wing suit in Switzerland in 2011.

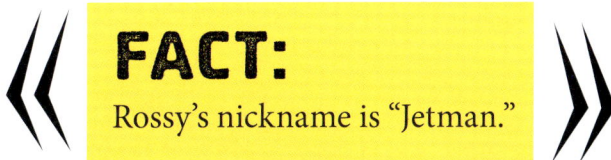
FACT: Rossy's nickname is "Jetman."

The Future of Aircraft

Some of today's aircraft designs will become popular aircraft in the future. Others won't be widely produced. But it's certain that technology advances will lead to future aircraft that seem impossible today.

Transportation experts think that someday people will own aircraft the way most people today own cars. These vehicles might offer people a safer choice for getting around than automobiles.

With a PAV, you could fly right over a traffic jam!

People have different ideas for how PAVs might look in the future. Some might have multiple propellers.

Future aircraft will continue to amaze and delight. They will go even higher and faster than the coolest rides up in the air today. If you could design one, what would you build? Where would you take it? The possibilities are endless!

GLOSSARY

altitude (AL-ti-tood)—the height of an object above ground level

combat (KOM-bat)—fighting between two or more forces

concept (KAHN-sept)—an idea for a new way to build or create something

prototype (PRO-tuh-tipe)—the first version of a new invention from which other versions are developed

radar (RAY-dar)—a device that uses radio waves to track the location of objects

solar (SOH-lur)—relating to the sun

stealth (STELTH)—the ability to move without being detected

technology (tek-NOL-uh-jee)—the use of science to do practical things

touchscreen (TUHCH-skreen)—a display that can be operated with the touch of a finger

wingspan (WING-span)—the distance between the wing tips of an airplane

READ MORE

Amin, Anita Nahta. *What Would It Take to Make a Jet Pack?* North Mankato, MN: Capstone Press, 2020.

Lanier, Wendy Hinote. *Flying Cars.* Lake Elmo, MN: Focus Readers, 2019.

Leigh, Anna. *How Drones Work.* Minneapolis: Lerner Publications, 2019.

INTERNET SITES

Fox News: Hoverbikes Are Now Real
https://www.foxnews.com/tech/hoverbikes-are-now-real

HowStuffWorks: How Flying Cars Will Work
https://auto.howstuffworks.com/flying-car.htm

Kids Discover: Drones to the Rescue
https://www.kidsdiscover.com/teacherresources/drones-uavs-rescue/

INDEX

B-52 Stratofortress, 9
Borschberg, André, 6

Carbon Fiber Jet Wing Suit, 26

drones, 12, 13

eVTOLs, 18, 20, 21
  Boeing eVTOL, 18–19

F-35B STOVL Lightning II, 14–15
flying cars, 22–23
  AeroMobil, 22
  Terrafugia Transition, 23

helicopters, 16–17
  CH-47F Chinook, 16
  S-97 Raider, 17
hoverbikes, 4, 24, 25
  Hoversurf S3, 24

Mackay, Dave, 10
Masucci, Mike, 10

personal air vehicles (PAVs), 20–21
  Airbus A3 Vahana, 21
  BlackFly, 20
Piccard, Bertrand, 6

radar systems, 15
Rossy, Yves, 26

sensors, 21
Solar Impulse 2, 6–7

technology, 4, 28

UAVs, 12–13
  MQ-8C Fire Scout, 13
  Predator C Avenger, 12

Virgin Galactic, 10, 11
VSS Unity, 10

X-51A WaveRider, 8–9